Summer 1981   Volume IV Number 2

I0190485

Paperback Quarterly

"Journal of
Mass-Market Paperback History"

Contents

Paperback Blurbs
  by Charlotte Laughlin & Bill Crider......................................3

Fires That Create --- The Versatility and Craft
of Harry Whittington
  by Michael S. Barson..13

Interview with Harry Whittington
  by Michael S. Barson..17

Modern Age Books and the John Esteven Mystery
  by Angela Andrews...29

Soft Cover Sketches: Lou Marchetti
  by Thomas L. Bonn...32

The European Paperback Prelude
  by Piet Schreuders..38

Reviews...46

Letters...52

Book Sellers..57

Paperback Quarterly Publications
Brownwood, Texas

Paperback Quarterly specializes in the history of mass market paperbacks. Its goal is to make the study of paperback history more comprehensive and reliable.

Paperback Quarterly features articles and notes dealing with every type (mystery, detective, science fiction, western, adventure, etc) and with every aspect of new, old and rare paperbacks.

Emphasis is placed on the historical research of paperbacks, their authors, illustrators, publishers and distributors, but the editors also invite contributions of bibliographical interest. In short, the only criterion for the editors' consideration is that the subject matter pertain to paperbacks.

Paperback Quarterly pays 1ᶜ per word (200-2000 words) for articles and notes. Payment also includes two copies of the issue in which your article appears.

Paperback Quarterly is published in Spring, Summer, Fall and Winter of each year with a subscription rate of $8.00 per year or individual copies for $2.95 each. Institutional and library subscriptions are $10.00 per year. Overseas rate is $12.00. All back issues are currently out of print.

All correspondence, articles, notes, queries, ads and subscriptions should be sent to 1710 Vincent St., Brownwood, Texas 76801. (915) 643-1182.

Ad rate card on request.

Published and Edited by

Charlotte Laughlin   Billy C. Lee

Contributing Editors

Bill Crider   Michael S. Barson
William Lyles   Thomas L. Bonn

Printer and Technical Advisor
Martin E. Gottschalk

Copy Editor
Judy Crider

Cover logo designed by Peter Manesis

Paperback Blurbs
by Charlotte Laughlin & Bill Crider

What are blurbs and where did they originate?
In his book THEREBY HANGS A TALE, Charles E. Funk
tells that the word "Blurb originated early in the
20th century--in 1907 to be precise. Gelett Burgess
authored a book called ARE YOU A BROMIDE?; and then,
as now, publishers gave booksellers at annual meet-
ings several copies of books for which a good sale
was anticipated. It was the custom to print on
the book jacket the picture of a young woman; so
to keep up with his competition, Burgess, a humor-
ist, borrowed from a Lydia Pinkham tooth-powder
advertisement the portrait of a sickly-sweet young
thing, drew in some flashing teeth and "otherwise
enhanced her pulchritude." For his text, he wrote
about the charms of "Miss Belinda Blurb." And so
the first cover blurb was born.

According to that great bibliographer and book
collector, John Carter, "blurb" is a "slang word,
borrowed from the vocabulary of the publishing
business, and irreverently applied to those puffs
or 'write-ups' with which booksellers sometimes
embroider their catalogues." Since mass-market
paperbacks are not sold via catalogues but via wire
racks in grocery and drug stores, the paperback
cover itself must provide its own puffery; and oh
how puffy those paperback cover blurbs can be!

Carter concludes his discussion of catalogue
blurbs thus: "Blurbs annoy some collectors, amuse
others, possibly influence a few. Good ones are
much harder to write than you think." Good paperback cover blurbs abound, and collectors of 40s and
50s paperbacks seem to be not at all annoyed by
them.

Paperback blurbs which were intended to be
strictly informational (about the author, publisher,
or number of copies sold) may have influenced the
original purchaser but seldom influence a collector.

On the other hand, blurbs which amused, titillated, or tantalized the original purchaser continue to amuse, titillate, and tantalize collectors. Those collectors among us who can read as well as look at cover pictures are at least as influenced by a good blurb as we are by pictures of gorillas, whips, and blacks. (Gorillas blacking whips? Blacks whipping gorillas? -- What sort of classification of paperback collectibility is that?)

Blurb readers classify paperback cover blurbs into at least five types: (1) Text-information blurbs, (2) Reputation blurbs, (3) Quotation blurbs, (4) Title-lead-in blurbs, and (5) Story blurbs.

Type (1) provides useful information but very little entertainment for the collector. It says such things as, "First publication anywhere," "Complete and Unabridged," "Specially revised and edited," "Abridged," or "Original title...." Hardback titles were often changed to something more graphic for paperback publication, but Lion Library #22 (THE WILD PLACE) does the opposite. The cover blurb lets the reader know that G. P. Putnam's hardback was titled GIANTS SHOULD BE GELDED.

The "Formerly titled" and "Abridged" text-information blurbs, by the way, were required by the Federal Trade Commission and are often found in minuscule print in an obscure corner. Not so, GIANTS SHOULD BE GELDED--that former title is proudly proclaimed. The reputation blurb may rely on the reputation of the publisher: "a genuine Pocket Book Mystery" or "A Bantam Western." It may tout the reputation of the author: "Earle Stanley Gardner writing as A. A. Fair," "Louis L'Amour's Classic," or "Louis Bromfield's best." Reputation blurbs may also exploit the fame of an author's previous work, a movie version of the story, or a classic with which the paperback is alleged to have something in common.

Dell #608, Emile Zola's THE HUMAN BEAST, carries the blurb "By the Author of 'NANA',"

5

whereas Ace D-16, GERMINIE by Edmond and Jules de
Goncourt claims that it is "Called the 'real origin'
of Zola's NANA." (That naughty NANA could really
sell books!) SERENADE, Signet #1153, carries the
statement above the title: "JAMES M. CAIN author
of The Postman Always Rings Twice." Dell #431,
BENJAMIN BLAKE, SON OF FURY, has the blurb "EDISON
MARSHALL author of 'YANKEE PASHA'." (What's so
great about YANKEE PASHA? you may be asking. Just
read its story blurb and you'll understand: "The
adventures of Jason Starbuck from the harbors of
Salem to the harems of Tartary....")
        The tie-in to a movie's reputation has always
been a popular paperback cover blurb. Dell #433
bears this one: "The story of the M-G-M picture
H. Rider Haggard's KING SOLOMON'S MINES, undreamed
of horror in Africa's darkest jungle, starring
DEBORAH KERR AND STEWART GRANGER." (This one is
particularly interesting in the way it plays on the
reputation of Haggard, who wrote the book the movie
was supposedly based on, but not the book Dell published. That one was done by Jean Francis Webb as
a novelization of the film, but you can discover
that only by a careful examination of the tiny
print on the contents page. Haggard's name is on
the title page, cover, and spine.)
        A blurb may also appeal to the reputation of
a celebrity who likes the book. In the case of
Gold Medal #240, THE DAMNED, by John D. MacDonald,
the celebrity endorsement was apparently considered
even more important than the cover picture of a
half-nude woman and man lying together in the
countryside. Slashed across that titillating picture is this blurb: "'I WISH I HAD WRITTEN THIS
BOOK!' -- MICKEY SPILLANE." Gold Medal #347,
HONDO by Louis L'Amour, appeals to the fame of a
movie star: "'Best Western I Have Ever Read' --
John Wayne." Of course Wayne had a vested interest:
he was starring as Hondo Lane in the movie version
of the book.
        Finally a reputation blurb may rely on the

7

ACE
D-16

TWO COMPLETE NOVELS 35c
Called the "real origin" of Zola's NANA

POPULAR LIBRARY
The Bubble Dancer Who Knew Too Much

524
GOLD MEDAL BOOK

Heaven was a girl named Paula—
her kiss—a passport to hell

A DELL BOOK
DELL
422

SECOND BIG PRINTING

COMPLETE AND
UNABRIDGED

Overnight the lovely
girl he married
became a
she-devil—
a tigress

The adventures of Jason
Starbuck from the harbors
of Salem to the harems
of Tartary . . .

POPULAR EAGLE BOOKS LIBRARY
The Story Of A Girl Who Wasn't Nice   **25c**

25c
DELL
BOOK
603

ERLE STANLEY GARDNER
writing under the name of **A. A. FAIR**

POPULAR LIBRARY
1391
Midnight Lovers in a 9 o'Clock Town

popularity of a fictional character: "a Kent
Murdock Mystery," "a Michael Shayne Murder Mystery,"
or "A bright and carefree story of the peerless
JEEVES and BERTIE...." (from Dell #393, P. G.
Wodehouse's THE CODE OF THE WOOSTERS).

Quotation blurbs may quote the book's characters, depicted in action on the book's cover.
Pocket Book #702, L. L. Foreman's DESPERADO'S
GOLD, sports this lovely piece of reasoning: "Don't
shoot boys. I'm too tired to duck!" Pocket Book
#2926, Ellery Queen's THE ORIGIN OF EVIL, pictures
a woman holding a handgun pointed directly outward
(toward the reader). "You're going to pay for
killing my father right now!" she threatens.

Other blurbs quote portions of reviews of the
book. Some of the quotations come from newspapers
hardly heard of outside of the hills, but no one
seems to care. It's those titillating, persuasive,
or laudatory phrases lifted from the reviews that
the blurb-writer is interested in. The blurb of
Popular Library #628, Jesse L. Lasky's CRY THE
LONELY FLESH, quotes that paragon of literary taste
the MEMPHIS COMMERCIAL APPEAL as saying of the book,
"Lusty...intense." One can only imagine the ful-
some adjectives represented by those little dots.
Who knows what else the APPEAL's reviewer said?
And who's ever going to check? (Speaking of para-
gons of literary taste, the editors of PQ are just
waiting for some paperback blurb writer to quote
from the BROWNWOOD BULLETIN, known locally as the
Brown Bull.)

Then there are the succinct quotations lifted
from reviews. Our favorite is "Good." We wonder
if the LOS ANGELES TIMES reviewer said "Good try
but a dismal failure." Just what did the reviewer
say was good about that book? Perhaps the ingenious
blurb writer didn't want us to know.

Blurbs which lead into the title of the book
are less common. Examples include Pocket Book
#1132 by Joe Rayter, "When a girl prefers men who
mix love with murder she's...ASKING FOR TROUBLE,"

and Bantam #359 by Leslie Ford which states, "He had to murder...ALL FOR THE LOVE OF A LADY."

The most entertaining blurbs, to us, are ones which tell about the story. Story blurbs give the reader a little better idea of what the book is about than do other kinds. Some story blurbs give a summary (and a laugh) as does Erskine Caldwell's KNEEL TO THE RISING SUN (MacFadden #50-231), which states: "In a world teeming with passion and violence, four women--a small town tramp, a young adulteress, a beautiful nymphomaniac and an aging prostitute--are caught in a web of tragedy."

Another great blurb, also of a Erskine Caldwell, title, appears on MacFadden Books #50-236: "A penetrating look at the violent men and women of the South--the brutal rapist, the lusting old man, the bold prostitute, the casual killer, the tantalizing small-town siren." After reading those two blurbs, we're wondering if there's any way to find out the identity of blurb writers. The same person must have written those two classics; and if we could find out who it was, we'd like to shake his hand.

There are shorter story blurbs, of course, like Basil Heatter's THE CAPTAIN'S LADY (Eagle Books #1): "The story of a girl who wasn't nice."

Many story blurbs are sexually suggestive. James Howard's I LIKE IT TOUGH (Eagle Book #46) proclaims "Sweet as sin and twice as dangerous." Mike Moran's DOUBLE CROSS (Popular Library #494) says "Velma's goal was every man in town." William Brown Meloney's MOONEY (Popular Library #1391) promises us "Midnight lovers in a 9 o'clock town." Joseph Landon's ANGLE OF ATTACK (Popular Library Giant #G117) states "All she had was his--For a night."

Some blurbs read like jingles, using alliteration, a poetic device which was a real speciality of Ace Books. For example: "Double Your Dough-- and Die!" (D-29, THE FAST BUCK, Ross Laurence); "It was either the gallows--or the goon" (D-147, MY PRIVATE HANGMAN, Norman Herries); "Head Over Heels

in Homicide!" (D-9, DECOY, Michael Morgan): "Corpse
Cargo on a Highway to Hell!" (D-43, DEATH HITCHES
A RIDE, Martin L. Weiss). Novel Library #29 sports
alliteration in title, author's name, and blurb:
Timothy Trent's ALL DAMES ARE DYNAMITE has the
cover blurb "A street-girl gives her real heart to
a guy in the gutters of hell."

Everyone has a favorite blurb or two, thanks
to the talents of those anonymous writers whose
labors are never credited. We'd like to thank them
for their ingenuity and for the fun they've given
us. The variety of paperback cover blurbs is end-
less, but here are a few we find particularly noteworthy:

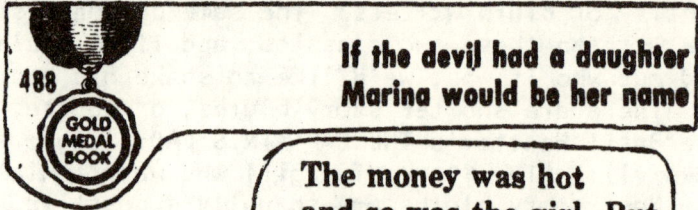

NL 29 — A STREET-GIRL GIVES HER REAL HEART TO A GUY IN THE GUTTERS OF HELL

488 GOLD MEDAL BOOK — If the devil had a daughter Marina would be her name

The money was hot and so was the girl. But it was cold-blooded murder just the same

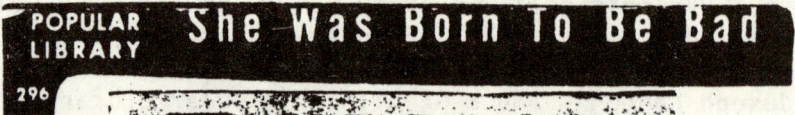

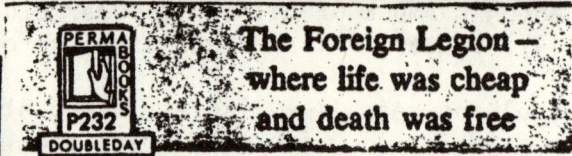

POPULAR LIBRARY 296 — She Was Born To Be Bad

PERMA BOOKS P232 DOUBLEDAY — The Foreign Legion — where life was cheap and death was free

ACE DOUBLE NOVEL BOOKS D-201 — They took their pleasure on the installment plan

Fires That Create --- The Versatility and Craft of Harry Whittington

by Michael S. Barson

In Harry Whittington's second book, SLAY RIDE FOR A LADY*, ex-cop Dan Henderson is sprung from prison, where he was sent on a trumped-up manslaughter charge, in order to track down Connice Nelson, the wife of the man who framed Dan and killed his brother Ray. Dan finds her in Hawaii; but before he can convince her to return with him, Connice is murdered. Worse still, it is made to look as though Dan did the killing. Dan grabs Connice's infant, leaves Hawaii, and heads back to Tampa and Harry Nelson, the man who framed him twice. Along the way Dan has to contend with the police, Nelson's mob, and a rival gang of hoodlums. In one memorable scene, Dan is knifed in the shoulder. As Dan begins to chase his assailant, the infant he is caring for begins to cry; this piece of narration follows:

> I jerked the knife out of my shoulder and threw it backhandedly across the room...The pain in my shoulder was the icy cold kind--if you've ever stuck an ice pick in your hand, you know how it was. It was cold and made me sick all over.
> Patsy was screaming as I ran toward the door... Roughly I thrust a cold bottle of milk into her mouth. The weight of my hand pushed her back in the bed, and she lay there still. I didn't wait to see if she was all right.
> I could feel the blood pouring down my arm as I ran across the room...It was agony, pulling that coat on over my arm, but I did it as I ran down the corridor....

Not even Mike Hammer ever stopped to feed a baby in the midst of chasing a killer!

---

*Whittington's first book was a western published in hard covers in 1946.

13

SLAY RIDE FOR A LADY was published in 1950.
Over the next three years, Harry Whittington had
the amazing total of 26 novels published as paperback originals, several of them in the then-
popular digest-size format. Some were hard-boiled
like SLAY RIDE; some were steamy backwoods romances;
some were lurid tales involving juvenile delinquents,
drugs, and/or sex. Actually, most of Whittington's
early work is moved along by the themes of lust and
greed, and what raw desire--either for a person or
for money--can do to one who yields to it. Whittington's characters are not so much motivated as
obsessed; they rarely stop to eat or sleep while
immersed in their tidal waves of emotions.

A Whittington character experiences passion in
its rawest state. There's Bernice Harper of FIRES
THAT DESTROY, who murders her blind employer for
$24,000, which she then squanders on a heartless
gigolo; Selma Mitchell of VENGEFUL SINNER, who goes
into shock after watching her husband being brutal-
ly murdered, only to escape from the asylum to
which she has been committed in order to catch the
killer herself; Mike Ballard, cop on the take, who
has to clear a condemned man of murder in order to
possess the man's wife; Greg Morris of HELL CAN'T
WAIT, who attempts to exact revenge for the death
of his wife by challenging the entire town of Koons
Mills; and Jake of BACKWOODS TRAMP, who tries to
recover $100,000 from a psychopathic killer who
has taken refuge in the Florida swamps. And these
are only a handful of the characters populating the
more than one hundred paperback original novels
that Harry Whittington has had published since 1950.
Whether writing under his own name, or the nom de
plumes of Hallam Whitney, Whit Harrison, Kel Holland,
or Ashley Carter, Whittington invariably manages to
communicate to the reader the naked emotions of his
protagonists, regardless of the outre predicaments
they find themselves in.

Consider the situation facing Joel Palmer of
MARRIED TO MURDER. A tough cop who, like Dan

Henderson, has been framed in order to get him off
the force, Palmer hires himself out to a rich woman
who wants him to pose as her deceased son-in-law--
a pose that, among other things, will require plas-
tic surgery. In order to start earning his money,
though, Palmer first has to dispose of a body that
his employer has been keeping in a freezer in her
apartment. The vivid description of Palmer's state
of mind as he carries out the operation is typical
of the intensity of emotion--in this case, fear--
with which Whittington infuses his characters:

> I was sweating. I was sitting in that
> tight little car with a hundred and
> eighty pounds of frozen meat on my lap
> and sweat was pouring out of me. It
> was running out of my hair down into my
> eyes.

If MARRIED TO MURDER is typical of Whittington's 1950s novels, it is hard to categorize his
work over the last twenty years. As Ashley Carter,
of course, he now is enjoying great success with
two series for Fawcett, "Falconhurst" and "Blackoaks," each of which concerns the plantation hijinks
which made MANDINGO so successful. But from 1969
to 1975, Whittington retired from the paperback
field in disgust, after a long string of unpres-
tigious and unremunerative film and television
adaptations, westerns, and nurse novels convinced
him that he was demeaning himself. He had become
a writer without honor in a market he helped to
create.

As the Eighties begin, however, Whttington
finds his star again on the rise. Although the
paperback field will never again see the predomi-
nance of the Gold Medal-type suspense novel of
the Fifties, of which Whittington was the acknow-
ledged master, this consummate professional has
adapted to the demands of today's marketplace.
During 1981 Whittington will see the next install-

ment in his "Blackoaks" series appear, along with
some romances (as Suzanne Stephens), a few entries
in Jove's "Longarm" adult western series, and an
historical saga or two. Whittington has endured--
and we are all richer for it.

Universal Giant #1 *Prime Sucker* (top) by Harry Whittington

Interview with Harry Whittington
by Michael S. Barson

MB: Your earliest paperback sales were to Jim Quinn's Handi-Books line. How did Quinn run his operation? Do you have any notions as to why Handi-Books folded at the end of 1951, just when the boom in paperback originals was beginning?

HW: SLAY RIDE FOR A LADY was my first paperback sale, made for me by writer William T. Brannon. Quinn also published my THE LADY WAS A TRAMP and THE BRASS MONKEY. Jim Quinn did not suggest any guidelines for his books. He was kind enough to tell Brannon that he bought SLAY RIDE because "it's the kind of novel I'd like to write."

I can only guess as to why Handi-Books folded. I would say Jim's decision to produce "odd"-sized paperbacks, which could not be displayed on the standard racks and so had to be stacked with the magazines instead, must have cost him. Perhaps distribution was poor because of this.

On the other hand, Jim Quinn was an excellent artist--often did his own covers and layouts (SLAY RIDE for one), as well as editing and proof-reading. There was every reason he should have succeeded. Before he went into publishing originals, he had reprinted some of the biggest names in suspense and modern novels. I was sorry to see him go.

MB: What were the pay scales like in those first days of paperback originals?

HW: Jim Quin paid me $750 advance on each of the novels he bought from me. Ace was a weird outfit and set their own pay rates. They paid me $1000 each for DRAWN TO EVIL and SO DEAD MY

17

LOVE! They paid as high as $2500 advance, but generally between one and two thousand dollars. They may have paid other writers less, others more; they were hard to pin down or keep track of. I don't know how honest they were in accounting for sales.

Venus, Original, Carnival and Phantom all belonged to Paperback Library. My deal with Paperback Library publisher Mauri Latzen was very helpful at that time. I could submit a three-page outline at any time and they would send me a check for $375, no matter how many other "ideas" they'd already bought! They paid an additional $375 when I submitted the finished novel, and $375 for each reprinting. Most of their books averaged between $1500 and $3000, counting reprints. Some made more. As near as I can tell from my lousy records, BACKWOODS HUSSY went into ten printings between 1952 and 1963.

Graphic Books bought three of my novels at $1000 advance on each. They were also printers and lithographers and I believe they used the books just to keep their presses busy.

MB: How did one go about submitting an original manuscript in those days, with so many houses eager for product? Who made the choice?

HW: I had an agent from 1950 to 1962 who decided arbitrarily where he would submit my work. Early in the '50s I wanted all of them (except the plot outlines I sold to Paperback Library) sent first to Fawcett, because they paid a $2500 advance and paid for each reprinting. They also allowed writers to keep all foreign, movie and other rights. Gold Medal was the prestige paperback line. After they bought FIRES THAT DESTROY from me in 1951, they got first look at most of my work.

18

MB: Was there much difference among the houses in the sort of product they wanted? Did any house ever specify that they wanted a more sexy sort of story than what you had submitted?

HW: I don't think there was much difference between publishers--and I had many! Ace never used sex in any overt way. Gold Medal thought they did--but looking back, we know there was no sex in any of those books!

MB: What factors persuaded you to try to crack the paperback market in the first place?

HW: It just happened that way. They were looking for writers who could produce swiftly and I was looking for publishers who paid promptly. I needed money to live and support my family. As you know, fewer than 400 writers actually support themselves from writing full-time. I did--for more than 30 years. I needed the "quick decisions--quick pay" of the paperback houses.

MB: Do you ever regret being categorized as a "paperback writer" rather than a "hardcover author"? Did this ever work against the success of any of your books?

HW: Unfortunately, the prestige was nil in the early days and the books died after a few weeks or months on the newstand shelves. But, on the other hand, many of the "trade" book writers of the same period who appeared in hardcover were paid less, lasted no longer, and faded after a summer or two. So, who knows?
    Naturally, I regret that a few of my books which were rated very highly by respected critics--such as Porgy winners PANAMA and RAMPAGE, and Spur winner SADDLE THE STORM-- never received more attention than they did.

19

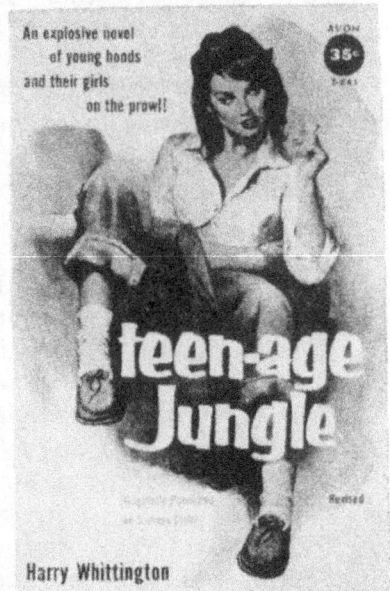

Paperbacks by Harry Whittington

It's like having children, sending them off
to compete in school where they excel in every
way, and then are failed by the authorities.
I may be prejudiced, but I believe than many
of the writers being touted, publicized and
lionized to instant fame in hardcover publici-
ty campaigns are going to flounder and fail if
they are ever put in direct competition with
paperback writers who have had to learn their
craft.

MB: Your novel RAMPAGE had an interesting premise:
the huge rock festival that causes all sorts
of conflicts within the town that has booked
it. How did you come to choose this subject?

HW: There had been several rock concerts--some
replete with riots--in Tampa. I got as close
to them as possible. My agent in Hollywood
and I worked on the music/film background.
        I don't think RAMPAGE sold nearly as well
as my Ashley Carter books. I thought Fawcett
gave RAMPAGE very poor exploitation and distribution. I liked it as a book.

MB: As Ashley Carter you have authored a number of
million-sellers in the historical romance cate-
gory. How do you research a book that's set
over a hundred years in the past?

HW: I use any materials I can find: old wills,
documents, books printed in the late 19th
century. The only recent histories I've used
have been on houses, furnishings, clothing,
guns and implements. I don't read other con-
temporary writers in this genre for many rea-
sons--primarily because I hope not to be influenced by any of them. Fan mail on Ashley
Carter has been heavier than on any of my
"Whittington" books, excepting THE DOOMSDAY
AFFAIR (THE MAN FROM U.N.C.L.E. #2),which drew

hundreds of letters from the 12-16 year-old group.[1]

MB: It's difficult to find many of the pseudony-
      mous works you wrote over the years, so I'm
      only hazarding a guess, but isn't the Green-
      leaf Classics imprint a porn line? The two
      novels you wrote for them, THE MEXICAN CONNEC-
      TION and NIGHTMARE ALIBI, don't sound like
      typical porn titles. Were they? STAR LUST,
      from B & B Library, does sound like a sex-
      oriented novel. Was it?

HW: None of the books you mentioned were written
      as porn, but they may have been spiced up by
      the editors. I don't know. They told me
      they wanted "books written your way, not ours."
      When a book of mine didn't sell to Gold Medal,
      Avon, Ace, Pyramid or Paperback Library, my
      agent usually sold it off where he could.

MB: The Gold Medal Falconhurst titles provide a
      biographical sketch of Ashley Carter, which
      reads as follows: "Ashley Carter traces his
      Deep South ancestry back at least nine genera-
      tions to Noble Worthington Hardee (1693-1743),
      who settled on the James River in Virginia.
      His great-great-uncle, Lt. Gen. Wm. J. Hardee
      CSA (1815-1873), was one of Lee's generals.
      His great-grandfather, Maj. Charles Seton
      Henry Hardee (1830-1927), was treasurer of the
      city of Savannah, Georgia, for forty years."
          Allowing for the obvious promotional
      value of having an author of Southern Histori-
      cals described in such a manner, exactly how
      much truth is there to the Carter/ Whittington
      pedigree?

HW: The biographical data on Ashley Carter is
      totally authentic, through my mother's family
      the Hardees of Savannah.

[1]Letter to Christopher Geist, June 1978.

Paperback Originals by Harry Whittington

SLAY RIDE FOR A LADY (Handi-Books #120, 1950)
THE LADY WAS A TRAMP (Handi-Books #131, 1951)
THE BRASS MONKEY (Handi-Books #138, 1951)
CALL ME KILLER (Graphic #36, 1951)
MURDER IS MY MISTRESS (Graphic #41, 1951)
MOURN THE HANGMAN (Graphic #46, 1952)
SWAMP KILL (Phantom Books #508, 1951) as Whit
     Harrison
SATAN'S WIDOW (Phantom Books #505, 1951)
MARRIED TO MURDER (Phantom Books #503, 1951)
VIOLENT NIGHT (Phantom Books #511, 1952) as Whit
     Harrison
FIRES THAT DESTROY (Gold Medal #190, 1951)
BODY AND PASSION (Original Novels #714, 1952) as
     Whit Harrison
SAVAGE LOVE (Original Novels #718, 1952) as Whit
     Harrison
FOREVER EVIL (Original Novels #708, 1952)
BACKWOODS HUSSY (Original Novels #723, 1952) as
     Hallam Whitney
SAILOR'S WEEKEND (Venus Books #153, 1952) as Whit
     Harrison
DRAWN TO EVIL (Ace D-5, 1952)
RAPTURE ALLEY (Carnival #918, 1953) as Whit
     Harrison
SO DEAD MY LOVE! (Ace D-7, 1953)
GIRL ON PAROLE (Venus Books #158, 1953);retitled
     MAN CRAZY (Zenith, 1960)
PRIME SUCKER (Universal Giant #1, 1953)
ARMY GIRL (Venus Books #194, 1953) as Whit Harrison
SHACK ROAD (Original Novels #731, 1953) as Hallam
     Whitney
VENGEFUL SINNER (Croydon #35, 1953);retitled DIE
     LOVER (Avon T-450, 1961)
CRACKER GIRL (Uni-Book #58, 1953)
SINNER'S CLUB (Carnival Books #923, 1953);retitled
     TEENAGE JUNGLE (Avon T-241, 1958)

SHANTY ROAD (Original Novels #742, 1954) as Whit
    Harrison
CITY GIRL (Original Novels #737, 1954) as Hallam
    Whitney
YOU'LL DIE NEXT! (Ace D-63, 1954)
THE WOMAN IS MINE (Gold Medal #366, 1954)
WILD OATS (Uni-Book #70, 1954)
BACKWOODS SHACK (Carnival #931, 1954) as Hallam
    Whitney
SADDLE THE STORM (Gold Medal #401, 1954)
THE NAKED JUNGLE (Ace S-95, 1955)
ONE GOT AWAY (Ace D-115, 1955)
SHADOW AT NOON (Pyramid #169, 1955) as Harry White
A WOMAN ON THE PLACE (Ace S-143, 1956)
WILD SEED (Ace S-153, 1956) as Hallam Whitney
DESIRE IN THE DUST (Gold Medal #611, 1956)
BRUTE IN BRASS (Gold Medal #595, 1956)
SATURDAY NIGHT TOWN (Crest #151, 1956)
THE HUMMING BOX (Ace D-185, 1956)
ACROSS THAT RIVER (Ace D-201, 1957)
ONE DEADLY DAWN (Ace D-241, 1957)
TEMPTATIONS OF VALERIE (Avon T-187, 1957) noveliza-
    tion of film
WEB OF MURDER (Gold Medal #740, 1958)
STAR LUST (B & B Library, 1958)
A TICKET TO HELL (Gold Medal #862, 1959)
HALFWAY TO HELL (Avon T-299, 1959)
BACKWOODS TRAMP (Gold Medal #889, 1959)
STRICTLY FOR THE BOYS (Stanley Library #72, 1959)
STRANGE BARGAIN (Avon T-347, 1959)
HEAT OF THE NIGHT (Gold Medal #959, 1960)
HELL CAN WAIT (Gold Medal #1044, 1960)
REBEL WOMAN (Avon T-403, 1960)
NITA'S PLACE (Pyramid G525, 1960)
A NIGHT FOR SCREAMING (Ace D-472, 1960)
CONNOLLY'S WOMAN (Gold Medal #1058, 1960)
STRIP THE TOWN NAKED (Beacon, 1960) as Whit
    Harrison
GUERRILLA GIRLS (Pyramid G600, 1961)
ANY WOMAN HE WANTED (Beacon #392, 1961) as
    White Harrison
DESERT STAKE-OUT (Gold Medal #1123, 1961)

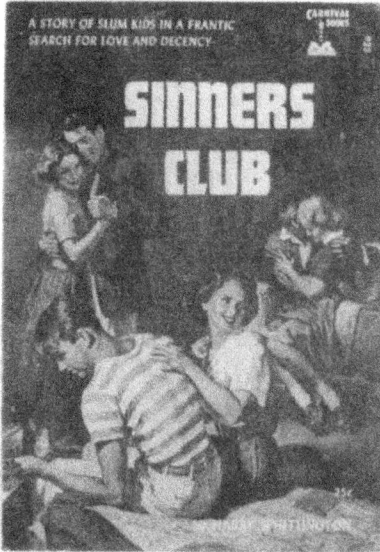

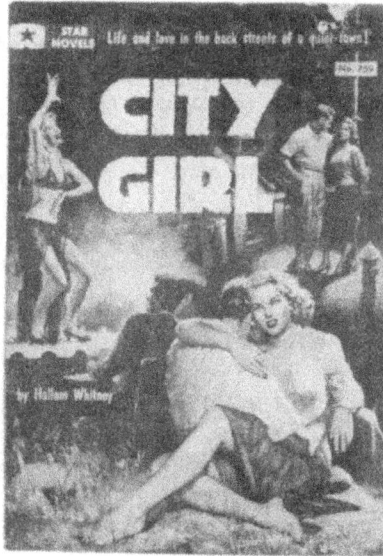

Paperbacks by Harry Whittington

JOURNEY INTO VIOLENCE (Pyramid G578, 1961)
THE YOUNG NURSES (Pyramid F680, 1961)
A WOMAN POSSESSED (Beacon #416, 1961) as Whit
    Harrison
A HAVEN FOR THE DAMNED (Gold Medal #1190, 1962)
GOD'S BACK WAS TURNED (Gold Medal #1134, 1961)
THE SEARCHING RIDER (Ace D-510, 1961)
A TRAP FOR SAM DODGE (Ace F-103, 1961)
WILD SKY (Ace F-148, 1962)
69 BABYLON PARK (Avon F-146, 1962)
HOT AS FIRE, COLD AS ICE (Belmont 90-269, 1962)
SMALL TOWN NURSE (Ace D-543, 1962) as Harriet K.
    Myers
DON'T SPEAK TO STRANGE GIRLS (Gold Medal k1303,
    1963)
DRYGULCH TOWN (Ace F-196, 1963)
PRAIRIE RAIDERS (Ace F-196, 1963)
PRODIGAL NURSE (Ace D-564, 1963) as Harriet K.
    Myers
CROSS THE RED CREEK (Avon F-219, 1964)
THE STRANGE YOUNG WIFE (Beacon #682, 1964) as
    Kel Holland
HIS BROTHER'S WIFE (Beacon #698, 1964) as Clay
    Stuart
THE TEMPTED (Beacon #714, 1964) as Kel Holland
HANG ROPE TOWN (Ballantine, 1964)
HIGH FURY (Ballantine, 1964)
SAMUEL BRONSTON'S THE FALL OF THE ROMAN EMPIRE
    (Gold Medal d1385, 1964) novelization of film
WILD LONESOME (Ballantine, 1965)
VALLEY OF SAVAGE MEN (Ace M-126, 1965)
THE DOOMSDAY AFFAIR (Ace G-560, 1965) THE MAN FROM
    U.N.C.L.E. #2
DOOMSDAY MISSION (Banner, 1967)
BURDEN'S MISSION (Avon, 1968)
SMELL OF JASMINE (Avon, 1968)
CHARRO! (Gold Medal r2063, 1969) novelization of
    film
THE MEXICAN CONNECTION (Greenleaf Classics, 1972)
    as Henri Whittier

Men couldn't keep their hands off Nona. It was a sweet way to die...

HOT AS FIRE
COLD AS ICE

A new novel by
HARRY WHITTINGTON

An earthy, warm-blooded woman and the man they said she could never have

HEAT OF NIGHT

HARRY WHITTINGTON

THE **BRASS MONKEY**

By
HARRY WHITTINGTON

Escape Me Never
A NIGHT FOR SCREAMING

HARRY WHITTINGTON

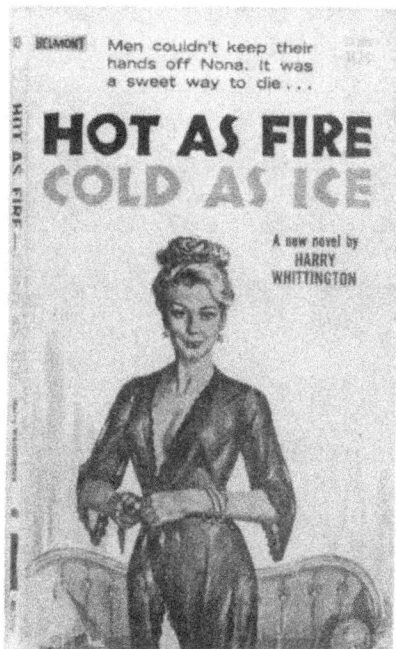

Paperbacks by Harry Whittington

27

THE GOLDEN STUD (Gold Medal, 1975) as Lance Horner,
    edited and rewritten by Whittington after
    Horner's death
MASTER OF BLACKOAKS (Gold Medal, 1976) as Ashley
    Carter
SWORD OF THE GOLDEN STUD (Gold Medal, 1977) as
    Ashley Carter
SECRET OF BLACKOAKS (Gold Medal, 1978) as Ashley
    Carter
RAMPAGE (Gold Medal, 1978)
PANAMA (Gold Medal, 1978) as Ashley Carter
SICILIAN WOMAN (Gold Medal, 1979)
TAPROOT OF FALCONHURST (Gold Medal, 1979) as
    Ashley Carter
THE OUTLANDERS (Jove Books, 1980) as Blaine
    Stevens
SCANDAL OF FALCONHURST (Gold Medal, 1980) as
    Ashley Carter
STRANGERS IN EDEN (Harlequin Super-Romance, 1981)
    as Suzanne Stephens
HERITAGE OF BLACKOAKS (Gold Medal, 1981) as
    Ashley Carter
LONGARM series (Jove, 1981-1982) #28, 32, 36, 40,
    44, and 48. as Tabor Evans

(Compiled with the aid of *Les Amis du Crime #5*, March 1980)

Modern Age Books
and the John Esteven Mystery
by Angela Andrews

At a time of increased interest in marketing
mass paperbound books in America, Modern Age Books
was founded in New York City in 1937 by Richard S.
Childs,who, with Samuel Craig and Louis Birk from
the Literary Guild and McGraw Hill respectively,
published and reprinted their Seal series of "good
books" in both soft and hard covers. Because of
competition from the American Mercury and other
rivals the pace had to be fast in order to break
even. Selling through book shops, chain stores
and newsstands, Modern Age also began a book service. Again there was competition not only from
Book-of-the-Month Club but from New York department stores with book clubs like Macy's Red Star
Book Club, which sold "five books for the price of
four." Perhaps the tone was too high or sales too
low but by 1939 Modern Age ceased publishing paperbound books. (See COLLECTING PAPERBACKS?, Vol. 3,
No. 3, p. 22, for an article on Modern Age Books.)

As a rare survivor of this shortlived period
GRAVEYARD WATCH by John Esteven is an interesting
example of Modern Age's paperbound books. As Seal
#40 it is one of only three mysteries: the other
two were #4 (MURDER STRIKES THREE by David MacDuff)
and #23 (DEATH SLAMS THE DOOR by Paul Cade). The
other original Seal Books and reprints are listed
inside its green paper dustjacket. As well as
mysteries (for only 25¢ or 35¢ in paper to 95¢ in
cloth) there were cook books, short stories, books
on current affairs and the biography of Mayor La
Guardia.

Of further interest, the dust jacket reveals
that cocaine, or "nose powder" circa 1938 is the
subject of GRAVEYARD WATCH: Irish sleuth, Patrick
Connelly, with a New York/Irish brogue goes on the
trail of a dope gang residing in a mansion of gin-
gerbread architectural style in King George's County,

Maryland..."on the low-lying shores of the Chesea-
peake."

Then comes the question: who is John Esteven?
The dust jacket notes also that "Esteven" is a
pseudonym for a writer and scholar of distinction
who likes to "dash off a murder story now and then
in an idle moment." Further research reveals that,
in fact, John Esteven is none other than Samuel
Shellabarger (1888-1954), a distinguished professor
from Princeton University and the biographer of
Lord Chesterfield and the Chevalier Bayard. Samuel
Shellabarger was also a historical novelist and
his knowledge of historical and social backgrounds
acquired from the places he visited on his many
travels became invaluable material for such romances
as CAPTAIN FROM CASTILLE, later a Twentieth Century
Fox film starring Tyrone Power as the Spanish captain accompanying Cortez into Mexico at the time
of the Conquest.

THE CUMULATIVE PAPERBACK INDEX shows that five
of Samuel Shellabarger's historical novels were
published in paperback by Bantam and also as Armed
Service Editions:

CAPTAIN FROM CASTILLE (Armed Service #854, ca.
        1945, and Bantam #A860, 1951.
THE PRINCE OF FOXES (Armed Service #1321, ca.
        1947, and Bantam #A973, 1952.
THE KING'S CAVALIER (Bantam #A1131, 1953.
LORD VANITY (Bantam #F1284, 1955)
TOBECKEN (Bantam #F1720, 1958)

Returning to John Esteven and mysteries,
however, the INDEX lists only WHILE MURDER WAITS,
Popular Library #343, 1951. As an "oversized"
paperback GRAVEYARD WATCH is not included in either
the INDEX or the PAPERBACK PRICE GUIDE. It remains
to be discovered whether or not other Esteven mysteries (THE DOOR OF DEATH, 1928; VOODOO, 1930; BY
NIGHT AT DINSMORE, 1935; and ASSURANCE DOUBLE SURE,
1939) were ever published as paperbacks, oversized
or otherwise.

As well as being "john Esteven, Samuel Shellabarger also wrote under the name Peter Loring to
author GRIEF BEFORE NIGHT, 1938, and MISS ROLLING
STONE, 1939. Again, it remains to be discovered
if any " eter Loring" paperbacks ever existed.

In any event, by recalling the early history
of Modern Age Books, the not so very mysterious
John Esteven mystery has been solved.

References:

CUMULATIVE PAPERBACK INDEX 1939-1959 by R. Reginald
    and M. R. Burgess, 1973
CURRENT BIOGRAPHY 1945: WHO'S NEWS AND WHY, 1945
THE PAPERBACK PRICE GUIDE, by Kevin Hancer, 1980
THE PAPERBOUND BOOK IN AMERICA, by Frank L. Schick,
    1958, pp. 62 and 125
NEWSWEEK, March 28, 1938, pp. 33-34, "Books: Price
    Cuts, Mass Production"

Seal Books

Soft Cover Sketches: Lou Marchetti
by Thomas L. Bonn

It is lunch time at the Society of Illustrators in midtown Manhattan. The walls of the third floor bar and dining room are decorated with sketches, advertising, and publishing artwork--proud samples of the membership's livelihood. The styles and compositions, like the grey-haired and blue-suited creators seated near them, have a familiar look.

Lou Marchetti, who also answers to "Gene" or "Geno," enters in a light-blue leisure suit. From first introduction, he dares you not to like him. For over 25 years Marchetti has made a living--almost exclusively--painting pictures on assignment for mass-market paperback publishers. He quickly summarizes his success: "I have an affinity for what people will buy. I've sold a lot of books."

Marchetti came to the United States from Italy at the age of 14. He found that his talent in art overcame many of the social and language barriers of his adopted country. Eventually it also overcame its financial barriers.

Throughout the interview, Marchetti never wanders far from his professional roots, pointing out positive and negative influences on his art as he recounts his career. "When I finished school I was a realist. I changed styles as the times demanded; I was not my own man for 10 or 12 years afterward."

Like so many young commercial artists of the early 50s, he was directly influenced by the realistic cover art of James Avati. But Marchetti says it was the very prolific cover artist Barye Phillips who "made a professional out of me. He was one of the greatest human beings I ever met."

When he was floundering in 1958, Marchetti recalls, another illustrator, Jim Meese, helped him find his way again. Former Ace Books art director Fred Gardener and Edward Rofheart, with Popular Library since its inception, gave Marchetti similar direction and support. "Rofheart is a fine art director because he builds up your confidence; he gets the best work out of his illustrators," says Marchetti.

Marchetti is highly critical of publishers and art directors who insist that an artist work to exact specification. This places such limitations on the composition of a cover that creativity is stifled. Such art directors lay everything out so that the artist's assignment is merely to fill in the empty spaces like a paint-by-numbers kit.

Dozens of interviews with publishing executives conducted prior to this meeting confirmed the universal law of mass market paperback publishing: The book won't sell if the cover doesn't work. And it follows that it is much harder for a cover illustrator to construct a satisfactory cover for a "big book" (one that a publishing house pays a large advance to acquire and is preparing a million dollar advertising and promotion budget to support its sale.) Corporate pressure to combine disparate ideas of what a particular "package" should contain can weigh heavily on the company's art director and filter down to the artist hired to do the cover, Marchetti explains.

Why do so many covers for blockbuster titles fail? Marchetti continues his explanation by saying that because of the enormous amount of pressure and advice, the artist may make compromises that tend to make a cover too conservative, or he may add gimmicks which make the cover a designer's nightmare. The best art work is often done for books that have moderate sales expectations because the pressures on an art department are minimal; the artist is free to try more creative ways to interpret the book's contents.

To those highly-paid art directors Marchetti pleads: "Don't show me your fears. If you do, you

33

Lou Marchetti

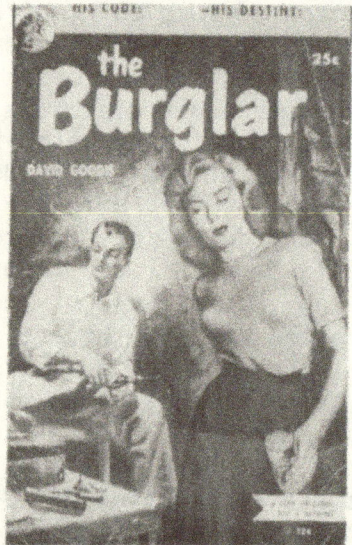

Paperbacks Painted by Lou Marchetti

destroy the good thing I have to offer."

Most illustrators acknowledge that, all things considered, drawing paperback covers offers more freedom than any other segment of commercial illustration. Restricted by the size (roughly 4" by 7"), by editorial content, and by design specifications set by the publisher, the artist is left to compose and illustrate in comparative freedom. "I happen to be a salesman who knows how to paint. And because I must be doing something right, I have been successful," Marchetti summarizes.

Under pressure, Marchetti can take a cover assignment over the phone. Within a day or two he can produce a finished cover which might take another artist two weeks or more to complete. "I am much faster than anyone else," he admits.

His years of experience and "affinity for what people will buy" give him enough confidence to work this way if the situation calls for it. As for quality, he observes, "At times I felt that I found a formula for the way covers should look. When I do a Gothic, it's the best you can get."

Marchetti is proudest of his title as the first illustrator of the modern Gothic cover. Today he will only do one as a special favor, but he estimates that through the years he has composed between 500 and 700 of them. Gothic novels have recently fallen victim to other women's reading categories, such as period and historical romances; but in their prime, Marchetti did seven or eight Gothic covers a month.

A few days after our interview, Marchetti sent me a copy of the book bearing his first Gothic cover, THUNDER HEIGHTS by Phyllis A. Whitney, published by Ace Books in 1960. Looking at it today, one sees that Marchetti incorporated all of the basic elements that eventually became clichés: fleeing virgin; dark, twisted landscape; castle looming in the background. But he lacked óne element: the light in the window. This requirement came a short time later. Editor-in-chief at Ace, Donald A. Wollheim, who later founded DAW

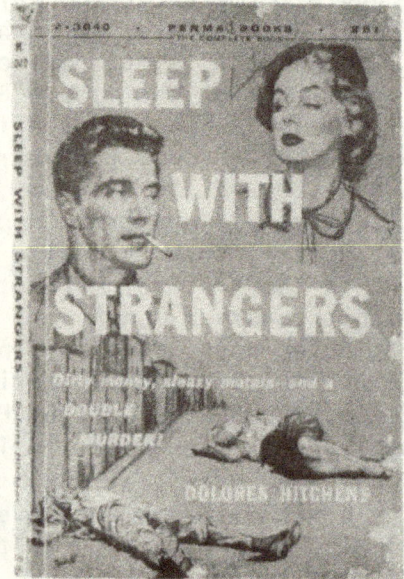

Covers Painted by Lou Marchetti

Books, takes credit as "the hand that lit that mysterious lamp." Wollheim found that sales increased by 5% when there was a beacon in the background of the cover illustration.

Toward the close of our interview, Marchetti revealed that he is thinking of quitting the confines of paperback illustrating to try his hand instead as a "gallery" artist. He observes that the paperback-cover painter is the only type of artist who can successfully bridge the gap between commercial work and gallery sales. Recent graduates of paperback covers--academic painters whose romantic realism descends from Remington, Pyle, N. C. Wyeth, and Rockwell--are earning $20,000 to $25,000 per painting in the galleries. "If you're not a realist, you don't get bought," Marchetti reminds me.

Paperback Quarterly currently needs articles about paperback publishers, authors, artists, individual books or series. All articles must be slanted toward paperbacks. We are particularly interested in short articles or notes, 200-400 words. Payment: 1¢ per word. Reporting time: 4 weeks.

The European Paperback Prelude
by Piet Schreuders

The "paperback" is not just a book which for one of many possible reasons has been published in a soft cover instead of a hard one. It is rather a type of book which for the purpose of appealing to a mass audience has been designed for the cheapest possible production and in a format most handy for mass display and reading comfort.

In this modern sense of the term, the paperback book made its first appearance in Europe, early in the 19th century.

Beginning in 1809, printer-publisher Karl Christoph Traugott Tauchnitz made a name for himself by issuing an inexpensive series of Greek and Roman classics, bound in paper covers. In 1837, in Leipzig, Christian Bernhard (later Baron) Tauchnitz, Karl Christoph's nephew, began to release his own series of paper-bound books: the TAUCHNITZ EDITIONS. Edward Bulwer, Lord Lytton, was the first author published in a Tauchnitz Edition; the second was Charles Dickens.

The series, consisting mainly of reprints of English and, later, American works, soon became popular in Europe. They were bought by Frenchmen and Germans who wanted to learn English, and especially by British travelers stocking up on reading material in Paris before boarding the Orient Express, preparing themselves for 48 hours in a cramped sleeping car on their way to Eastern Europe. They even found a market in South America and the Middle East.

Officially, Tauchnitz Editions were not distributed in English-speaking countries. The agreement not to sell them in Britain was, in fact, a gentleman's agreement with no legal standing, as the current international copyright conventions did not yet exist.

(From *Paperbacks, U.S.A.: A Graphic History, 1939—1959.* Published in the U.S. by Blue Dolphin Enterprises, Inc., 4887 Ronson Court, Suite E, San Diego, CA 92111)

Baron Tauchnitz wanted his relationships with authors to be mutually beneficial: he paid them royalties although he was not legally obliged to do so; and at the end of the century, his son, Christian Karl Bernhard, was making regular visits to England to maintain contact with such authors as Dickens, Disraeli and Thackeray.

The "look" of these earliest of early paperbacks was not very impressive. Like French books, the pages were uncut, so that anyone who actually wanted to read a Tauchnitz Edition had to do the cutting himself, winding up with a volume of ragged-edged pages in his hands. The pages themselves were too wide, the type was too small, the lines of print were too long to be comfortably readable. Still, the books were successful: by the 1930s there were some 5,000 titles in the series, an average of about one new title a week for almost a century!

Except for minor adjustments of the cover typography, there were no signs of a move to adapt to changing tastes in book design and editorial interest. This failure made the company vulnerable to an attack on the quasi-monopoly which it had enjoyed for about a century.

Then in 1932 a new competitor appeared on the scene with a new paperback series of British and American reprints, based on the same system of uniform format, low price, regular monthly releases and market restrictions, but with a number of changes which made the books more attractive to readers and booksellers alike.

That competitor, THE ALBATROSS MODERN CONTINENTAL LIBRARY, was organized and managed by British publisher John Holroyd-Reece and German publisher Kurt Enoch. Its editor was Max Christian Wegner, a former Tauchnitz executive. Financially backed principally by Sir Edmond Daves (with Kurt Enoch as minority partner), the main office was in Hamburg at Schauenburgerstrasse 14; the editorial office was in Paris at 37 Rue Boulard, and there

was a temporary production office in the Via
Milasso in Bologna. Like the Tauchnitz Editions,
the Albatross books were officially only to be
distributed on the European Continent; in each
volume were printed the words, "Not to be introduced into the British Empire or the U.S.A." An
average volume cost 1.80 German Reichsmarks, or
12 French francs, or 9 Italian lira. Four new
titles were published each month; early authors
included James Joyce (his DUBLINERS was the very
first Albatross), Alduous Huxley, Sinclair Lewis,
Hugh Walpole, Virgina Woolf, A. A. Milne and
Edgar Wallace.

Special new features of the Albatross series
included a completely new overall book design by
Giovanni Mardersteig, at that time art director
of Mondadori printers. He created a new format
of 11.1 x 18 cm (4 1/3" x 7"), which permitted a
longer type page and established a width that
easily fit into a coat pocket. He used economical
and readable type faces, designed an attractive
standard cover pattern and a stylized picture of
an albatross as a colophon. He also used better
paper.

Another important feature was Albatross'
system of color coding the covers (red, blue,
yellow, green, orange, silver and gray), indica-
ting the genre of each folume. A short blurb
about the author and the contents of the book in
English, French and German inside the cover also
made it easier for the customer to choose and the
seller to sell.

In addition to these new features, the close
British connections, the location of the editorial
office in Paris instead of Leipzig and generally
a better adaptation to the new literary trends
developing outside the more and more politically
isolated Germany resulted in editorial offerings
more appealing to the market than those available
from Tauchnitz.

Consequently, with rapidly increasing

Albatross Books

Tauchnitz Editions

Albatross sales and popularity, Tauchnitz's weakening position led to discussions of a merger of the two companies. Objections by the Nazi regime to a takeover of the old German firm by British interests were resolved by an arrangement according to which the printer of Tauchnitz, Oscar Brandstetter in Leipzig, purchased the Tauchnitz Company but turned over all editorial, design, and marketing activities to Albatross. For all practical purposes, this meant a merging of Tauchnitz into Albatross except for the printing.

As a result, all new features used in the production of Albatross books were gradually also applied to Tauchnitz. The size of the Tauchnitz books became identical with those of Albatross; and a modern, standardized cover design and a new, eye-catching Tauchnitz colophon made Tauchnitz books equally appealing. Editorially, an attempt was made to give the Tauchnitz Editions a more conservative, traditional tone in contrast with Albatross' more modern and even experimental choices.

This arrangement was well on its way to success when, in July 1935, Penguin Books, a new British paperback reprint series, appeared on the market. In its technical aspects it began as a somewhat cheaper version of Albatross. All books were of a standard size (the same as that designed by Mardersteig!); they were released periodically in groups; there was a standard design for all covers, including a bird colophon; and a color code for the covers' indicated genre. The typography and paper, however, were inferior; and there were two other important differences. The reprint licenses for Penguin Books included the British Empire and home market, permission which permitted substantially larger print runs and, consequently, substantially lower sales prices: a Penguin Book cost only sixpence.

The guiding force behind Penguin was Allen Lane, who worked for The Bodley Head, a hardcover publisher. At first, The Bodley Head was not enthusiastic about Lane's suggestion of an English-language paperback series; such series had appeared on a small scale in England in the early years of the 20th century and even during the 19th century, specializing in cheap reprints and mainly available at W. H. Smith kiosks. Most of these publishing ventures were short-lived, and the books themselves were of generally poor quality.

Allen Lane perservered, though, and eventually succeeded in establishing Penguin Books, Ltd. His biggest early triumph was a thousand-book order placed by the Woolworth's chain, which at that time sold only articles priced at sixpence. There is a story that, just as he was about to be sent away from Woolworth's without an order, the director's wife happened into the office where Lane and her husband were meeting. Her husband asked her, as a typical British consumer, if she would buy Penguins at Woolworth's. She looked over Lane's samples, said yes, and the rest is history.

Twenty Penguin titles were published during the company's first year; 50 the second year. Fifty new titles a year became Penguin's average, even through most of World War II (although only 33 appeared in 1941 and 37 in 1942). Furthermore, Penguin Books, Ltd. started several additional lines. The first of these, Pelican, was a series of educational books covering scientific subjects. The first Pelican, published in the spring of 1937, was George Bernard Shaw's THE INTELLIGENT WOMAN'S GUIDE TO SOCIALISM AND FASCISM. Shaw wrote two new chapters expecially for the Pelican edition, and this was the first time that Penguin published original work, as opposed to strictly reprints. It was not to be the last.

In the autumn of 1937, as the threat of a second European war became grimmer and grimmer, Penguin introduced a series of books dealing with the current world situation. These volumes, mostly originals, were called Penguin Specials.

The first title, GERMANY PUTS THE CLOCK BACK, came out in November, 1937; 18 Specials were published in 1938 and 30 in 1939. They sold so well that, when paper rationing began, Penguin was able to claim and receive a large share of England's available stocks.

Several other new series appeared during the war years, such as King Penguins (deluxe editions with colored illustrations and hard covers, selling for a shilling), Penguin Hansards (dealing with specialized, war-related subjects), Puffin Picture Books and Puffin Story Books for children, and Penguin Handbooks.

The characteristic style of the Penguin covers--horizontal colored bands at top and bottom (such as, for example, orange for works of fiction) with the words "Penguin Books" in the top band and a drawing of a penguin in the bottom band--was developed by Edward Young, a 21-year-old employee of The Bodley Head who "dabbled" in sketching. He drew the original Penguin penguin himself, after a special study trip to the London Zoo.

From the beginning, the orange Penguins were fiction, the green were thrillers, the blue travel and adventure stories, the cherry-red were biographies, and the yellow miscellaneous. Later, a light-blue cover was introduced for Pelicans, along with grey for books on world affairs, red for plays, and purple for collections of essays.

Tauchnitz began to lose business when Albatross entered the marketplace, and Penguin and Pelican took sales away from both of them. That was the situation when deteriorating political conditions in Germany necessitated further reorganization of the Albatross/Tauchnitz concern. In 1936, Kurt Enoch left Germany and moved to Paris. There and in London he organized two new companies (the Continenta SRL in Paris and the Imperia Book Co., Ltd. in London) as bases for new publishing and distributing activities abroad. At the same time, Max Christian Wegner resigned his position

and moved back to Germany, where he acquired all
of Enoch's German publishing and distributing
businesses. The editorial activities of the
Albatross concern were taken over by the office
of Holroyd-Reece in Paris. After a short inter-
val, during which Enoch continued sales of Albatross and Tauchnitz to markets outside Germany,
that function too was turned over to the Paris
office.

When the war broke out, Enoch left for London,
where he sold French books for a time. Meanwhile,
in Leipzig, the Tauchnitz-Albatross concern came
under new management, which made sure that a
series of German-language Tauchnitz books was
published during the war years: the Deutsche
Tauchnitz-Reihe. Where the English Tauchnitz
Editions could not be sold in Britain or America,
each volume of this wartime German series carried
the legend: "Nur zum Verkauf ausserhalb Gross-
deutschlands" ("Only for sale outside Greater
Germany").

After the war, Wegner made several attempts
to revive Albatross and Tauchnitz. New offices
were opened in Paris and London; and, just as in
1932, Albatross books were again printed by
Mondadori in Verona. They were also printed in
Leyden (The Netherlands), in Paris and in Scot-
land. The Tauchnitz New Series began in 1947,
published in Hamburg and printed in Heide and
(both in West Germany). At the beginning of the
50s, Bernhard Tauchnitz Verlag moved to Stuttgart
(still in West Germany) and had a firm in Verona
handle all printing. But international copyright
conventions and legal problems plagued both
Tuachnitz and Albatross, and neither survived.

Important publishers not only in their own
right, Tauchnitz and Albatross served also as the
forerunners for what later became known as the
"paperback revolution"--the worldwide production
and distribution of inexpensive mass-marketed
books, universally and widely available.

Books About Books

Paperbacks U.S.A.: A Graphic History, 1939-1959. by Piet Schreuders. Blue Dolphin Enterprises, Inc., 1981. $10.95.

Hardboiled America. by Geoffrey O'Brien. Van Nostrand Reinhold Company, 1981. $16.95.

Cumulative Paperback Index 1939-1959. by Robert Reginald and M.R. Burgess. Gale Research, 1973. $40.00.

What those of us who cannot read Dutch have been waiting for is here: the English edition of PAPERBACKS, U.S.A. And the prose lives up to the expectations we formed while drooling over the excellent cover reproductions in the Dutch edition. More than 100 paperback covers are reproduced in full color, and several hundreds in black and white. The pictures we knew to be crisply reproduced and representative of the development, styles, and genres of paperback art. Now we know that the text is equally crisp and informative. PAPERBACKS, U.S.A. is by far the best book about paperbacks that I've seen. Only CUMULATIVE PAPERBACK INDEX equals it in usefulness to the collector and student of paperback history.

As the subtitle suggests, PAPERBACKS, U.S.A. is primarily concerned with paperback art and artists; but don't let the title fool you. It also contains a wealth of information about paperback publishing and chronology in general.

Part One is "The History of the Paperback." It contains sections on the European and American preludes to mass-market paperback publishing; and individual histories of Pocket Books, Avon Books, Penguin Books, Popular Library, Dell Books, Bantam Books, and Signet Books. The discussions of individual publishers include quotations from art directors and artists interviewed by Piet Schreuders. His primary research in interviewing these people makes the entries much more interesting than standard rehashes of dates and titles. Another original feature is the "Graphic Description" which appears at the end of each publisher's entry. These descriptions summarize the chronological development of each publishing house's artwork, including colophons, cover format and design, endpaper color and illustration, and interior illustration.

Part One also includes a section on "Books in Wartime," outlining the early Victory Book Campaign, in which Pocket Books and Avon Books participated; Overseas Editions, Armed Services Editions, Infantry Journal Books, and Superior Reprints and Bantam Books.

Another section of Part One is a quick rundown of paperback publishers which came on the scene after the close of World War II: Graphic, Checker, Pyramid, Lion, Fawcett, Ballantine, Ace, and Berkley.

The final section of Part One is a good explanation of the development of the mass-market distribution system for paperback books in America.

Part Two focuses on the paperback covers themselves. Schreuders discusses legal controversies about paperback covers, noteworthy trends in cover art, the role of art directors, the steps involved in producing a cover, influences on paperback cover art, the recognition (or lack thereof) accorded paperback cover artists, and statements from some of the artists.

Part Three (Appendices) is so full of information that it could easily comprise a separate reference work. The first appendix is "Year by Year," giving not only the pertinent information about paperback publishing and art that occurred in each given year but also the general historical and cultural background that puts the development of paperbacks in perspective. For example, the entry for 1939 reads as follows:

The New York World's Fair opens. Frank
Sinatra makes his first record, and John
Steinbeck's THE GRAPES OF WRATH is a best-
seller in hardcover. The Soviet Union
invades Finland, the German Army marches
into Poland and war breaks out in Europe;
the United States declares itself neutral.
German-publisher Kurt Enoch leaves
Europe for New York, where the British
frim, Penguin Books, sets up an American
branch office headed by Ian Ballantine....

Each year is also profusely illustrated with
black and white cover reproductions of paperbacks
published in that year.
- The alphabetical "Overview of American Paperback Publishers" outlines seventy publishers from
Ace to Zenith, giving the first five titles of each
publisher and sometimes the first five titles of
different series done by the same publisher.
The "Who's Who in Cover Art," while not complete, gives short biographies of 160 paperback
artists of the two decades covered by the book.
Many entries include a photograph of the artist and
reproductions of some of the covers he did.
Finally, the bibliography is annotated and the
index is thorough.
Adding to the appeal of the book is the fact
that it is physically attractive and well-made.
Measuring 5 5/8" x 9", it is bound in heavy, flexi-
ble, glossy cover stock printed in full color. The
endpapers, front and back, contain reproductions of
paperback colophons. The cover endpapers are printed in red and black and the free endpapers in gray.
The title page features the line drawing that appeared on the title page of GENTLEMEN PREFER BLONDES
(Popular Library #221). Overall, PAPERBACKS, U.S.A.
is the best $10.95 investment a paperback collector
can make....
BUT WAIT! Subscribers to PAPERBACK QUARTERLY
don't have to pay $10.95. M.C. (Bunker) Hill, book
dealer and contributor to both PAPERBACK QUARTERLY

and COLLECTING PAPERBACKS?, is serving as whole-saler for the subscribers of both periodicals. His wholesale price is $6.57, plus $1.75 postage; so for $8.32 you can have a copy of PAPERBACKS, U.S.A. delivered to your door. Send your check to Bunker Books, P.O. Box 1638, Spring Valley, CA. 92077.

---Charlotte Laughlin

★ ★ ★

HARDBOILED AMERICA is a visually fine book, with its beautiful Norman Saunders jacket painting, 49 color reproductions of paperback covers, and numerous black-and-white reproductions. The author, Geoffrey O'Brien, a poet of some note, doesn't try to define what he's discussing, however. He simply tells about "all those books that orbit near the undefinable quantity" which he refers to as the hardboiled novel as it appeared in paper covers.

The book is marred by this lack of definition and by O'Brien's jargon that implies that the reader should somehow mystically intuit what the subject of the book really is. He writes of the early paperback industry as contributor to cultural change in the following passage:

Many people contribute to such shifts:
each writer, as he plugs himself into
the collective mythology and filters
it through his own consciousness; each
painter, as he sets out to depict scenes
from that mythology, like a more ancient
artist sketching according to a preor-
dained format the hieratic emblems of
some Gospel or Sutra.

The prose seems to be some odd cross between Marshall McLuhan and Omar Khayyam--a far cry from the "tough realism" O'Brien praises. It seems that he, too, suffers attacks of what he refers to as the "English Department of the soul," which afflicts so many of us; but the book improves greatly after the first 16 pages.

The lack of crisp definition of subject matter allows him to bring in writers such as Erskine Caldwell and Calder Willingham as well as the expected ones like Chandler and Hammett. And O'Brien doesn't dwell only on major figures. He mentions such lesser lights as Morton Cooper and Wenzell Brown, as well as underrated writers like Jim Thompson and David Goodis. He talks about covers as well as the contents of paperback books from the point of view of someone who loves them and has read them and collected them. The book's style is subjective and readable, on the whole, though readers may disagree with some of his statements. Bill Crider, for one, thought his comments about Cornell Woolrich were exactly on target--"he [Woolrich] wrote in a bloated purple prose that thuds like overemphatic movie music." But O'Brien's remarks about Jim Thompson were disappointing because it appears that O'Brien hasn't read nearly all of Thompson's books. Those he's read, however, he covers admirably.

HARDBOILED AMERICA isn't without errors, such as several references to cover artist "Walter Papp," but little things like that shouldn't detract from your enjoyment. Besides, the color pictures of paperback covers are beautiful.

★ ★ ★

CUMULATIVE PAPERBACK INDEX 1939-1959, which has been out of print for some time, is now available in a second printing. Unfortunately, the errors in the first printing have not been corrected and the price has increased to $40; but it is still an indispensable reference work for collectors and bibliographers. Reviewing the first printing of the INDEX in the summer 1979 issue of PAPERBACK QUARTERLY, Bill Lyles refers to CPI as "the bible" for paperback collectors, adding that "Until Reginald produces a revised edition...it is invaluable."

Good news from Reginald is that an extension
of the paperback index through the decade 1959-
1969 is still in preparation. It should be com-
pleted in 1982.
---Charlotte Laughlin

"*Make dust our Paper, and with rainy eyes,*
Write sorrow on the bosom of the earth."

—SHAKESPEARE

Letters

Dear Billy,

Just received the latest PQ and wanted to drop you a line about a couple of things....I must comment on the Bloch interview which really caught Bloch's zaniness perfectly--he really talks like that! It was hilarious. The issue is terrific as usual; the dust-jacket article was of special interest to me as well....

Best, Jan Landau

Dear Billy,

Many thanks for the latest PQ, which I'm still reading. Here are some additions to paperbacks with dust jackets: Bantam 26, 44, 67, 315, 360, and 462. Piet Schreuders also discusses paperback dust jackets in his book, PAPERBACKS, U.S.A. The Manesis article looks very good....

Best, Bill Lyles

Dear Billy,

While I was rummaging through a box of paperbacks (looking for something else entirely), I came across an item to be added to the list of paperbacks with dust jackets on page 28 of the current PQ. It is Bantam #26, NET OF COBWEBS, by Elizabeth Sanxay Holding, (March 1946). This book has another interesting feature: an endpaper illustration (signed Morgan), incorporating a blurb-like caption.

Best wishes, Bob Briney

PB Quarterly:---

Your latest issue (Spring '81) provokes a response.

First of all, why not admit the facts and change the title to PAPERBACK 'ZINE--PUBLISHED IRREGULARLY. Always, or at least as long as I've

been subbing, the Spring ish arrives in August or
some such. The cover dates are a farce! [*A peri-
odical by any other name would be as late, so why
not quit your griping about semantics? C.G.L.*]

Cover price ($2.95 per) is getting up there.
So are, I suppose, printing costs. The fact that
you pay your contributors is, I suppose, a part of
that price. [*Your grasp of the obvious is truly
amazing. Those suppositions are masterpieces of
deductive reasoning. I'm hoping for further enlightenment from you on the subject of economics.*]

The John D. MacDonald and Robert Bloch interviews couldn't have been too much better. [*How much
better could they have been, Jeff? Surely you have
some insights you would like to share with the fans.*]
All of the interviews have been good, but these were
two of the best, as far as Mike's really being able
to get the subject to open up and say something.

The subject of payment/money is starting to
get a little tedious and tiresome, at least to me,
and I'm a part-time mail order dealer, who can, like
all of us, sure use the cash! Let me clarify that:
I like money, as does any dealer; sure, but I also
really enjoy the paperback book field. It's a lot
more fun than comics were in the late '60s-early
'70s when they began to have some price movement.
Runaway inflation and sky-high prices will ruin
this hobby for the fans; I hope that doesn't happen.
From my viewpoint, it is kind of nice to see books
rise some in price---but when a book should sell for
$10-$15, and major and/or comic book dealers are
asking $25 and don't get it---well, I personally
think that's a good sign. I'll stop right there
and would like to hear contrasting opinions, as far
as that subject goes. [*Would that he had been true
to his word and stopped right there; but, no; this
letter goes on and on. I said that I hoped for
some enlightenment on the subjects of economics,
but I wasn't enlightened by the above. And what in
the Spring PQ provoked all this talk about money?*]

As for the rest of the issue---that is, the
articles/etc. that I'd like to say something about

---here, you're going to get a little negativism, I'm afraid. To wit (for want of a better phrase):--

The James Bond article---plenty of cover repros, a lot of info, yes. But, a lot of it is info that any reasonably knowledgable pb collector already knows. Do you mean to honestly tell me that the writer did not already know or assume that most pb collectors were not aware that pre-Signet editions of James Bond pb's are worth "a lot" of $$ and were not desirable additions to one's collection? [*The sentence immediately preceding reads exactly as it appears in the original; and for the life of me, I can't make any sense of it; I think there are too many "not"s in the sentence--but which one(s) is to be left out? Nowhere in the Bond article is monetary value mentioned, so what's with the quotation marks around "a lot"? And if the pbs are worth a lot of money why are they not desirable additions to a pb collection? Note: This is the letter writer's third mention of money, and he's not through yet! C.G.L.*]

Same goes for M. C. Hill's article. Again, I'd like to use dollar value as a standard of collectibility. Any dealer, major or minor, who can get much over 75¢ out of a fine or better Shadow pb with a Steranko cover (or even for the ones without Steranko covers) has done QUITE well, in terms of sales. [*"The subject of payment/money is starting to get a little tedious and tiresome, at least to me,..." And to me, too, Jeff. C.G.L.*] As for the info---I question Hill's research. A lot of the comic-related info could quite easily have been swiped from a Price Guide or comic fanzine. I don't say that the facts are false [*Facts never are.*] ---merely that the info is hardly something moderately knowledgeable collectors do not already know. [*Why do you question M. C. Hill's use of secondary resources such as Price Guides or fanzines? The purpose of most research is to compile and synthesize information from various sources into one article with a unique slant. C.G.L.*]

The last lines of the above paragraph are mainly the bones I have chosen to pick. In comparison, most of us did not know nearly so much about MacDonald or Bloch. [*Good Heavens! Is there more than one of you out there? C.G.L.*]

Manesis' article on the dust-jacketed pb's, though written in a super-hip '70s-'80s style, was also ultra-informative. [*Why the conditional "though"? C.G.L.*]

The articles on the PAPERBACKS USA exhibition and the "note" by Avati were good, considering length and the fact that not all of us could be there in Holland. [*I'm beginning to panic--"all" sounds as if there are a whole lot of your kind running around loose! But perhaps there's hope; if you haven't yet invaded Holland, maybe I could immigrate there. And by the way, what was so good about the length? C.G.L.*]

All tnings considered, Spring '81 was one of your better issues, with some flaws. And, when some of those flaws get corrected, the 'zine will be even better. Let's not play down [up?] to newcomers constantly and tell vets what we already know; hit a more middle-type ground, and concentrate on articles that do not retell what is, to a lot of us, common knowledge. [*"A lot of us"? I'm terrified that somewhere in Ohio this letter writer, man or Alien that he may be, is cloning himself.*]

I for one would like to see some more info on Jim Thompson. I've read the majority of his books, except for the very-hard-to-find hardcovers like HEED THE THUNDER; and this man is or was a tremendous writer! (Prob, past tense, as I believe he was born approx. 1917). [*Don't people live past 65 anymore? If not, I'd better tell my grandmother because she was born in 1898, and she's a lot livelier than I am! C.G.L.*] As I acquired most of the books on loan from another person and/or sold the copies I had after reading them, I don't feel qualified to write an article.

(That's about it. How much of this are you going to edit, if you print it?) [I thought it would be a kindness to you and other PQ readers to print your first sentence followed by an ellipsis and then your last sentence. But you asked to have all your decadence paraded in black and white for all posterity to see, so here it is. C.G.L.]

Very Truly Yours,
Jeff Patton

Book Sellers

The following people sell paperbacks. Many mail out booklists on a regular basis and all are knowledgeable paperback biblio-philes. For specific wants write directly to the addresses below and please include S.A.S.E.

BILL & PAT LYLES
77 High St.
Greenfield, MA 01301
(413) 774-2432

SCOTT OWEN
P.O. BOX 343
Moraga, CA 94556

GRAVESEND BOOKS
Box 235
Poconopines, PA 18350

Anthony Smith
1414 Lynnview Dr.
Houston, Texas 77055

PCI
P.O. Box 1308
Hawaiian Gardens, CA 97016

JEFF MEYERSON
50 First Place
Brooklyn, N.Y. 11231

JACK IRWIN
16 Gloucester Lane
Trenton, N.J. 08618

FANTASY ARCHIVES
71 Eight Ave.
New York, N.Y. 10014

BILL LIPPINCOTT
Dunbar Hill Rd.
North Anson, ME 04958

MICHAEL BARSON
117 Crosby St.
Haverhill, MA 01830

JAN LANDAU
Rt 2 Box 293
New Castle, Virginia 24127

FAMILY PAPERBACKS
4016 Central Ave. N.E.
Minneapolis, MN 55412

SIGN OF THE UNICORN BOOK SHOP
604 Kingstown Rd.
Peace Dale, RI 02883

ED KALB
3227 E. Enid Ave.
Mesa, Arizona 85204
(602) 830-1855

JEFF PATTON
3621 Carolina St., N.W.
Massillon, OH 44646

McCLINTOCK BOOKS
P.O. Box 3111
Warren, OH 44485

FANTASTIC WORLDS BOOKSTORE
4816 A Camp Bowie Blvd.
Fort Worth, Texas 76107

BUNKER BOOKS
P.O. Box 1638
Spring Valley, CA 92077
(714) 469-3296

PAPERBACK PARADISE
468 Centre St.
Jamaica Plain, MA 02130

BARRY & WALLY PATTENGIL
Rt 3 Box 508
Waco, Texas 76708

THE OLD BOOK STORE
210 E. Cuyahoga Falls Ave.
Akron, OH 44310

MURDER BY THE BOOK
194½ Atwells Ave.
Providence, RI 02903

GALE SEBERT
Sebert's Books
Leivasy, WV 26676

LUCILE COLEMAN
P.O. Box 610813
North Miami, FL 33161

PANDORA'S BOOKS LTD
Box 86
Neche, ND 58265

MOSTLY MYSTERIES BOOKS
398 St. Clair Avenue East
Toronto, Ontario M4T 1P5

THE ODYSSEY SHOP
1743 S. Union Ave.
Alliance, OH 44601

LARRY RICKERT
R.D.1 Box 56C
Augusta, NJ 07822

JOHN DA PRATO
61 Puffer Lane
Sudbury, MA 01776

ABRA-CADAVER
The House of Mystery
110 Dunrovin Lane
Rochester, N.Y. 14618

REMEMBER WHEN SHOP
2433 Valwood Pkwy.
Dallas, TX 75234

PD BOOKS
P.O. Box 2132
Pawtucket, RI 02861

RON CZERWIEN
7289 W. 173rd Pl.
Tinley Park, IL 60477

MIKE LOVINGER
2146 Thistlewood
Burton, MI 48509

KEITH & MARTIN BOOK SHOP
310 W. Franklin St.
Chapel Hill, N.C. 27514

TOM NIGRA
865 Diane Court
Woodbridge, NJ 07095

If you are a bookseller and would like your name and address printed in "Book Sellers," please drop us a line. Please tell us if you sell paperbacks by mail and/or have a retail store. If you are interested in selling *Paperback Quarterly*, please write for our wholesale rates.

Bunker Books
P.O. Box 1638
Spring Valley, CA 92077

Wanted to buy: Avon Paperbacks, I'll pay $5 fair, $10 good, $20 fine

# 38	Chandler	Big Sleep
63	Chandler	Five Murderers
88	Chandler	Five Sinister Characters
104	Irish	If I Should Die
162		Avon Book of Crosswords
219	Chandler	Finger Man

Avon Murder Mystery Monthlies

# 7	Chandler	The Big Sleep
9	Stout	The Red Box
19	Chandler	Five Murderers
27	Woolrich	The Black Angel
28	Chandler	Five Criminals
31	Irish	If I Should Die
42	Irish	Borrowed Crime
43	Chandler	Finger Man
47	Clark	The Blond, The Gangster

$5 fair, $10 good, $20 fine

$5 for a copy of John Tebbel's
Paperback Books: A Pocket History

Red Arrow Paperbacks $5 each
# 1	Christie	13 at Dinner
3	Rhode	Murder in Praed St.
7	Riis	Yankee Komisar
9	Beeding	Seven Sleepers
10	Mason	Captain Nemisis
12	Moore	Windswept

1 (1960)   Ellery Queen Anthology $5

Dell 10ᶜ #   11,26,33 $30 each

www.ingramcontent.com/pod-product-compliance
Lightning Source LLC
Chambersburg PA
CBHW021224020426
42331CB00003B/455